COWES WEEK

THE ISLE OF WIGHT COWES WEEK SAILING REGATTA

DAVE WILLIS

HALSGROVE

First published in Great Britain in 2010

Text copyright © Dave Willis 2010
All Photographs © Dave Willis/ mountainsportphoto.com

British Library Cataloguing-in-Publication Data
A CIP record for this title is available from the British Library

ISBN 978 0 85704 012 1

HALSGROVE
Halsgrove House,
Ryelands Industrial Estate,
Bagley Road, Wellington, Somerset TA21 9PZ
Tel: 01823 653777   Fax: 01823 216796
email: sales@halsgrove.com

Part of the Halsgrove group of companies.
Information on all Halsgrove titles is available at: www.halsgrove.com

Printed and bound by Grafiche Flaminia, Italy

CONTENTS

RNLI crews and boats at Cowes Yacht Haven.

DEDICATION TO THE RNLI

The 2009 Cowes Week sailing regatta chose the RNLI, the Royal National Lifeboat Institute, as its official charity and of course it could hardly have chosen a more apt beneficiary. The RNLI depends on volunteers across the UK and Republic of Ireland who are united by a willingness to commit time and energy to a cause about which they are passionate. It is because so many crew-members, shore helpers, fundraisers and others are *volunteers* that funds can be spent on first-class lifeboats and equipment that has saved countless lives at sea since 1824.

A percentage of the profits from this book will be donated to the RNLI and I hope that in buying this book you will not only enjoy a glimpse of the spectacle that is recognized as one of Britain's great sporting traditions and a world class event but will also have made a small but important contribution to continuing the amazing and selfless life-saving work that RNLI volunteers do for us all.

Thanks.

Dave Willis
2010

INTRODUCTION

THE ISLE OF WIGHT COWES WEEK SAILING REGATTA: A SHORT HISTORY

Cowes Week is a British sporting institution. It is one of the longest running and most successful sporting events we have and has become a highlight of the British sporting summer. It has been held in early August every year since 1826, except during the two world wars.

Traditionally, Cowes Week takes place after Goodwood and before the Glorious Twelfth (the first day of the grouse shooting season) presumably so the well-heeled yacht owners of yesteryear wouldn't miss out on either.

In 1826 a race for a "Gold Cup of the Value of £100", was held for just seven yachts under the flag of the Royal Yacht Club (which later became the Royal Yacht Squadron in 1833 by command of King William IV). The next year, 1827 King George IV presented a cup (the King's Cup, presented at every subsequent event until 1939) and the event became known as Cowes Regatta. This was run as a three-day, then a four-day, event and quickly became part of the social calendar.

The early 1900s saw Cowes Regatta grow in stature as the classic 23 metre yachts competed along with 19 and 15 metre boats followed by the legendary J-class yachts of the 1930s.

After the war, from 1946, other Cowes and mainland clubs organised racing either side of the three days and the regatta grew in size and popularity. The King's Cup was replaced by the Britannia Cup, presented to the Royal Yachting Association by King George VI in 1950 and by 1953 the event had grown to nine days of racing, with each club running its own event with its own sailing instructions, racing marks and even start and finish lines.

In 1957 the first Admirals Cup, organised by the Royal Ocean Racing Club, was held during the week, which attracted competitors from around the world and opened the regatta to an international audience. The RORC is again hoping to re-start the Admirals Cup in 2011.

In 1964, HRH Prince Philip (Admiral of the Royal Yacht Squadron and a regular competitor), suggested Cowes Combined Clubs was formed to run and organise the regatta. This body represented the seven clubs involved in managing the racing (Royal Yacht Squadron, Royal London Yacht Club, Royal Thames Yacht Club, Royal Southampton Yacht Club, Royal Southern Yacht Club, Island Sailing Club and Royal Ocean Racing Club) and Cowes Town Regatta Committee. The Royal Yacht Squadron line became the accepted start line and a single set of sailing instructions and racing marks for the week would be used, replacing the confusion of individual club racing instructions, markers and start lines that had served in the past.

Sponsorship of the event had become increasingly important as Cowes Week grew in size and complexity and in 1995, following two years during which Cowes Week was supported by the County Council, Skandia took over as sponsors of the event. Around the same time, Cowes Week Sponsorship Limited was formed in order to manage all the sponsorship rights of the event. In 1998 the Royal Corinthian and Cowes Corinthian Yacht Clubs joined Cowes Combined Clubs and became responsible for organising the first committee boat starts. 2004 saw the 40th anniversary of Cowes Combined Clubs and was marked by a move into a new purpose-built Regatta Centre, which was officially opened by HRH Prince Philip.

The regatta has come a long way since 1826. With over 1,000 boats in up to forty different handicaps, one-design and multi-hull classes racing every day for eight days, the regatta is a unique mixture of classic and ultra-modern designs with several classes still racing after more than 50 years; Dragons, Flying Fifteens, Redwings, Seaview Mermaids, Solent Sunbeams, Swallows, Victories and XOD's. New classes are being introduced as they increase in popularity. The Laser SB3s for example, have been the largest class of the regatta for the past few years.

Cowes Week attracts over 8,500 competitors, ranging from Olympic and world-class yachtsmen and women to weekend sailors – all racing together and watched by over 100,000 visitors to Cowes. One of the most enduring traditions of Cowes Week is the spectacular fireworks display, which has taken place on the final Friday of Cowes Week since the very first years.

Even though Cowes Week was without a major sponsor in 2009, a legacy of the economic climate, the event went ahead anyway and was as always, hugely successful and enjoyed by competitors and spectators alike. Indeed the regatta is such an indelible fixture on the British (and international) sporting scene that it is taken for granted that it will continue to thrive and inspire all who love sailing, competition and the ocean for years to come.

Opposite: Classic yacht Mikado, (IRC class 6 racing) is the oldest yacht racing at Cowes Week 2009, leading a Sigma 38 into Cowes, close inshore in light winds.

Racing signal flags fly on the flagstaff at the Royal Yacht Squadron

CHAPTER 1
SAILING REGATTAS: A BRIEF GUIDE TO RACING

For the uninitiated, sailing races at a regatta can be an impossibly confusing spectacle. Dozens of boats, weaving this way and that around markers and buoys in what can appear to be a very haphazard fashion. And not just a single class of boat either; Different designs, sizes and configurations intermingle, jibe and tack around one another as they jostle for position and wind. So perhaps an introduction to racing would be useful.

Racing groups
All together, the racing boats are known as the fleet. The fleet is divided into two groups; The white group (open day-boat classes) and the black group (larger boats with cabins).

Start lines
Unlike other competitive racing, sailing cannot use a single start line because of the changing nature of wind and tide conditions. Nearly all racing at Cowes Week starts from opposite the Royal Yacht Squadron and a signal displayed on the flagstaff outside the RYS indicates the direction of start – a green signal for west and a red signal for east. The start line itself is formed by lining up the main RYS flagstaff with the diamond shape on the roof of the RYS castle. An outer mark or shipping buoy forms the other end of the "line". White group boats start close inshore whilst black group boats normally start further offshore. There are so many classes racing at Cowes that starts can go off at 5 minute intervals, alternating between the inner and outer start lines for up to two hours.

The courses
Course setting is tricky. Weather conditions and tidal ebb and flow will dictate what is sensible and courses are set daily for each class using modern, sophisticated computer software. The courses are set using racing marks, of which there are about 100 to choose from in the Solent. There may be up to 36 classes racing each day but courses are set to make sailing safe and manageable, avoiding classes colliding with one another.

Finishing
Black group and white group boats finish at different locations. Black group boats normally finish at the Royal Yacht Squadron (good for spectators) whilst the smaller white group day-boats usually finish offshore, east of Cowes by a committee boat. However, if the wind dies in the afternoon it's sometimes necessary to shorten the course and finish at a committee boat or a turning mark. It might seem that sailing is an odd spectator sport in that it all takes place off-shore but at Cowes spectators are often treated to the unusual sight of dozens of sleek, fast yachts under full sail and spinnaker, jostling for position close inshore alongside The Green as they race for the finishing line at the "Squadron".

The Daring class (white group) finish at the Royal Yacht Squadron with canon fire at Cowes Week 2009.

Committee boat Windy tows a line of Victory class boats back to the start line after a false start in near windless conditions.

The traditional, brass starting canon at the Royal Yacht Squadron, shining in the sun.

Class 1 IRC (black group) boats race in light winds as they approach Cowes, inshore along The Green. Spectators gather on the grassy banks to watch the spectacle of dozens of racing yachts competing close inshore.

13

Crowds line the beach to watch Extreme 40 racing at Cowes Week.

Extreme 40 racing at Cowes Week. The course is set just offshore along the promenade, which allows crowds to watch the action easily and enjoy the racing.

Club members watch the racing from the balcony of the Royal London Yacht Club House at Cowes. The RLYC is one of the Cowes Combined Clubs that now organise Cowes Week.

Spectators watch as the starting canon and signal flags are used at the Royal Yacht Squadron during the morning's racing.

The XOD class (white group) off the start line during racing at Cowes.

Opposite: Black group IRC class 8 boat Hemi finishes past The Green, framed by colourful villas overlooking the promenade at Cowes.

CHAPTER 2
THE WHITE GROUP: INTRODUCING THE WHITE GROUP CLASSES

The fleet known as the white group is made up of open day-boats, in other words boats without cabins that would normally be used for recreational day use or racing; dinghies to the layman!

The white group has a diverse range of boats within the fleet and many of them have been in use for a very long time and have real historic value. Some of the fastest boats are ultra modern designs made with high tech materials and using the latest sail geometries and rigging patterns.

Sailing in these classes is always competitive, tight and full of drama (and raised voices!). Many sailing clubs race single design fleets so the sailors are often club-mates and are all too familiar with each other's tactics which makes for exciting and combative sailing.

Opposite: **REDWING CLASS BOATS AT COWES WEEK**
The beautiful and distinctive Redwing is the oldest competitive sailing fleet in the UK. Designed by Charles Nicholson, originally there were only 27 wooden boats built between 1897 and 1937 but GRP versions have been in production since 1987. Seven of the original wooden boats still sail out of Bembridge.

FLYING FIFTEEN CLASS BOATS
AT COWES WEEK

Designed in Cowes in 1947 by Uffa Fox, the International Flying Fifteen is a fast, competitive two-man keelboat. There are 40 competitive fleets in the UK and at least 20 more worldwide.

DARING CLASS BOATS AT COWES WEEK

The Daring was designed by Arthur Robb, based on his 1956 Olympic silver medal winning, 5.5 metre yacht Vision. The class is unique to Cowes with 36 boats sailed by crews of three.

LASER SB3 CLASS BOATS AT COWES WEEK

Launched in 2002, the Laser SB3 designed by Tony Castro is a modern, fast racing boat sailed by a crew of three or four and is one of the most popular classes at Cowes Week with over 95 boats competing.

SQUIB CLASS BOATS AT COWES WEEK

Squibs are very popular little boats, designed in 1967 by Oliver Lee, with over 500 of them regularly racing in fleets around the country. The Squib is particularly well suited to junior sailors with a 13-year-old skipper competing in a squib at the 2009 Cowes Week regatta.

XOD CLASS RACING AT COWES WEEK

The XOD class have been racing in the Solent area since 1911. These one-design, all wooden, classic boats are favoured by many ex-national, world and Olympic champions, so racing is fiercely competitive. There are over 70 boats in the fleet, which also makes racing quite crowded!

CHAPTER 3

THE BLACK GROUP: INTRODUCING THE BLACK GROUP CLASSES

The black group consists of cruisers and cruiser-racers. Some of them are rated according to a strict international rating system to allow differing sizes and types of boat to compete on equal footing. The biggest class, Class Zero, is reserved to the very biggest "round the world" type racing yachts like the IMOCA Open 60s, whilst IRC classes 1-6 are occupied by other boats with the smallest cruisers in class 6. The exact IRC class rating that a boat has is difficult to know because of the complex formula used but it allows them all to race competitively together.

Also racing in the black group are the ISCRS class 1 & 2 boats. The Island Sailing Club Rating System is designed for boats that race occasionally and have participated in the Round the Island race this year. Most are crewed by friends and family and are raced for fun. Then there are a small number of classes like the J/109s, Sigmas and Sonatas that compete together in a one-design class.

Opposite: *IRC class racing at Cowes Week 2009.*

Class Zero racing yacht Ran at Cowes Week.

IMOCA Open 60 class Hugo Boss at Cowes Week 2009. These are the superstars of modern ocean racing – the biggest boats with an overall length between 18.5m and 30.0m and an IRC rating of 1.400 or higher. These boats come from all over the world to compete at Cowes and use the regatta as preparation for the internationally famous Fastnet race that starts on the last Sunday of Cowes Week.

Beau Geste HK, a Class Zero racing yacht at Cowes, the largest of the Class Zero boats competing in 2009.

Class 6 IRC racing in light winds at Cowes Week.

IRC racing at Cowes.

IRC class crews race in light winds approaching Cowes, close inshore.

IRC racing at Cowes, On-Deck Racing's Beneteau First 40.7. These are very popular boats for "sailing experience" days and are often used for corporate and race charter in the UK, competing in the Round the Island race and the Fastnet race.

ISCRS

Crew on board an ISCRS class yacht at Cowes Week. Small cruisers raced for fun by friends and families can be rated as ISCRS class and compete on Saturday with the chance of winning a Cowes Week trophy.

J/109

J109 class racing at Cowes Week. Designed by Rod Johnstone of J/Boats, this very popular class has been very successful in the UK with over 100 boats competing around the country.

CHAPTER 4

EXTREME 40S: THE FORMULA 1 RACERS OF THE SAILING WORLD

Extreme 40s are unique, high performance catamarans. The hulls are carbon fibre, designed to race in sailing's Grand Prix events, close inshore which makes the race series very exciting to watch for spectators. The Extreme 40s are among the fastest wind-powered craft on the planet and accelerate at unbelievable speeds. Extreme 40s can reach speeds of 35 knots on flat water in winds of around 20-25 knots. Designed by Yves Loday, the boats are built by TornadoSport and race in the iShares Cup at Cowes with a variety of famous names from the yachting world. The iShares Cup Extreme 40 Sailing Series is a six-event European sailing circuit that features the world's best Olympic, America's Cup, Round the World and solo sailors competing in this adrenaline-fuelled event with a crew of 4+1. The "+1" is a non-participating member, which means that crews are often joined by sponsors or other celebrities; Mike Golding, Dame Ellen MacArthur and Ben Fogle all competed on Extreme 40s at Cowes in 2009.

Opposite: *Friends and families make a picnic day of it on the beach for Monday's iShares Cup Extreme 40 racing in good weather, though light winds.*

Extreme 40 boat, Oman is sponsored by the Sultanate of Oman's Ministry of Tourism and is one of two Extreme 40s campaigned by Oman Sail.

Holmatro, skippered by Mitch Booth at full tilt off Egypt Point.

Ecover, skippered by Mike Golding gets a flying start despite fairly light winds in the iShares Cup race on Monday afternoon.

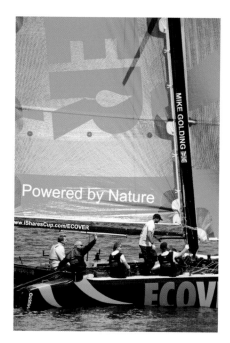

Above: Mike Golding's crew wave to the crowd as the Extreme 40 boats are paraded prior to the start of racing.

Right: Ecover and iShares battle it out alongside Egypt Point.

Opposite: Close racing between Mike Golding's Ecover, the Groupama boat and Shirley Robertson's iShares Extreme 40 off Egypt Point.

Spectators watch the iShares Cup Extreme 40 racing from Egypt point.

iShares team boat is skippered by double Olympic gold medallist Shirley Robertson and crewed by New Zealand's Jonathan Macbeth and fellow Brits Hugh Styles and Nick Hutton.

Rounding the racing marks at either end of the course can result in some very close sailing and near misses as each boat vies for wind and water position. These extremely light, carbon fibre boats don't need much wind to accelerate at a phenomenal rate.

Team "Oman Sail" line up in formation as they parade in front of spectators before the start of Monday's iShares Cup at Cowes.

The Oman Sail boats in tandem just off The Green, at Cowes.

Above: *Extreme 40 sailing fans take the opportunity to mingle with the crews at the landing stages and grab photos and autographs. The Extreme 40 iShares Cup series has really opened up high end racing to spectators who wouldn't otherwise get much chance to see this level of competitive sailing at close quarters.*

Right: *A local kayaker appreciates the action from as close to the racing line as he dares to paddle. The close-in nature of Exteme 40 racing makes an exciting spectacle for onlookers who can watch all the action from the beach and cheer on their favourite crews.*

In the iShares "village" entertainment and public bar area, racing scores and information boards keep the fans informed as to what is happening out on the water and a public address system provides a running commentary as racing gets under way. Spectators can relax with a drink, meet old friends and enjoy the great weather as the fast and furious boats blast past the bar area.

CHAPTER 5
BLACK GROUP RACING

There are over 105 trophies presented to black group boats throughout the week at Cowes, with most days seeing up to 16 cups, plates, salvers and bowls awarded throughout the fleet. The trophies are awarded on a daily basis to the winning boat from each class and overall trophies are awarded to the top three boats in each class over the duration of the entire week's sailing.

Amongst the honours there are a number of very prestigious cups with long histories. The Queen's Cup was first presented to the Royal Southampton Yacht Club by Queen Victoria in 1897 in the year of her Diamond Jubilee and was thereafter raced for on the opening day of Cowes Week each year. Curiously it was lost (!) in the early 1900s but rediscovered in 1937, in a second hand shop in Cardiff by a club member – some find! The cup is raced for by IRC class 1 boats. The New York Yacht Club Challenge Cup is also an IRC class 1 trophy and was first presented in 1951 to mark the 100th anniversary of the America's Cup with the intention of encouraging overseas yachts to compete at Cowes. The Britannia Cup is another famous trophy with royal connections and much sought after by IRC class 1 skippers. It was presented to the Royal Yachting Association (RYA) in 1950 and first won by Group Captain RJS Barton at the helm of *Taiseer IV* in 1951.

Opposite: *Competing in a 41-mile challenge for the Queen's Cup, one of the most prestigious prizes awarded during the week, is Johnny Vincent's* Pace, *a TP52, which took second place both on the water and on corrected time.*

Opposite & right: *The Italian STP65 Luna Rossa competed against three other maxis in the first IRC Class Zero race around the Isle of Wight and on corrected time came first with* Ran *runner-up and* Beau Geste *third.*

Karl Kwok's brand new Hong-Kong based IRC 80 Beau Geste, competed against three other maxis in the first IRC Class Zero race around the Isle of Wight in a steady 18-knot south-westerly to win by seven minutes over British mini-maxi Ran, owned by Niklas Zennstrom.

Niklas Zennstrom's JV 72, Ran competed well at Cowes and went on to become the winner of the Fastnet Trophy for best corrected time in IRC overall, for the 2009 Rolex Fastnet race.

The 12 metre yacht Italia ITA 7 competing in the class 1 racing at Cowes.

The Red Funnel ferry IKEA, steams across the racing line providing an added challenge to all the boats racing off Cowes throughout the day.

One of the top rated boats in IRC racing is Derek Saunders' Farr 60 Venom.

J109s with spinnakers flying, battle for the line just off Egypt Point at the end of the day.

The beautiful William Fife-built classic yacht Mikado, racing in IRC class 6. This Clyde Linear 30 design owned and skippered by Royal Yacht Squadron member, Sir Michael Brigg, was built in 1904 and was the oldest yacht racing at Cowes Week in 2009.

Class 1 racing in very light winds can lead to very tight finishes with dozens of boats jostling for position and flying every inch of sail they carry.

Above: Magic Mix is a Pharo X-41 yacht racing in IRC class 2, seen here making the most of brisk winds off Egypt Point.

Left: Pieter Vroon's brand new Ker 46, Tonnerre de Breskens, racing in the Solent for the Britannia Cup.

The Artemis Challenge at Cowes Week was contested by a number of leading yachts including Artemis Ocean Racing, skippered by British yachtswoman Sam Davies, and the BT IMOCA 60, skippered by Frenchman Seb Josse, who had enlisted the help of Dame Ellen MacArthur as crew. They eventually took first place, ahead of Pindar in second and Artemis The Profit Hunter in third, seen here later in the week starting the Fastnet race.

Dee Caffari's Open 60 Aviva, approaching The Needles at the start of the 2009 Fastnet race, which is held immediately after Cowes Week on Sunday. Dee is the first woman to have sailed solo non-stop round the world in both directions.

CHAPTER 6
WHITE GROUP RACING

For many sailors the white group races are the real core of Cowes Week. It may be a world famous event but at its historic heart it's still a local sailing regatta and the smaller open day-boat classes make Cowes Week accessible to many club sailors campaigning small sailing dinghies. That's not to say that the racing is any less exciting to watch, much less to compete in – indeed the white group races are very often the hardest and closest fought of all the week's sailing. The classes are very evenly matched and because these day-boats are economic to own and sail, all crews have a fighting chance of winning honours.

Historic boats grace the white group classes even more than in the black group. 2009 was the 75th anniversary of the Victory class with 20 boats competing and the oldest (*Kestrel*) built in 1934. The distinctive Redwings have a long history of racing at Cowes too. The original, wooden boats were built between 1938 and 1950, by Camper and Nicholson Ltd, to a design by Charles Nicholson and still race out of Bembridge on the Isle of Wight. And the XOD class – X One Design – was originally built by Alfred Westmacott, of Woodnutts Boatyard at St Helen's on the Isle of Wight. He was also responsible for the *Seaview Mermaid*, *Solent Sunbeam* and the *Victory*, all day-boats that are still racing in the Solent. The XOD class remains the largest class in the white group with over half the fleet competing (over 70 boats), which is something of a tradition at Cowes.

Opposite and pages 71-77:
XOD class racing in light winds and heavy skies ensures all boats are flying jibs and as
much sail as possible through the Solent chop, and crews work hard to maximise their opportunities.

Pages 78–80: Constant sail tuning and running repairs are critical in the closely matched XOD class, where any boat has an equal opportunity to win and tactics, knowledge and a bit of luck all play a part.

Pages 81–86: *With brighter conditions and stronger winds the XOD class boats sprint around the course with racing every bit as close and no quarter given.*

The Squib is the largest keelboat class in the UK and is sailed by a 2-person crew. The Squib class fielded an entry of 18 boats at the 2009 Cowes Week, with one boat, Aquabat helmed by 13-year-old Freddie Warren-Smith doing particularly well against an experienced fleet.

Pages 88–91: *The Daring class is unique to Cowes with over 30 boats in the current fleet. The strict one-design rules ensure that owners compete in identical boats even to the point where hulls can only be scrubbed once every two weeks – so you can't just throw money at your boat in order to win races!*

The classic Redwing fleet becalmed in the Solent and praying for wind. The Redwing's distinctive burgundy-coloured sleek sail is easily identified. During the 103 year history of Redwings, Ratsey & Lapthorne have made the red sails but in 1959 the original cotton fabric ran out and synthetic materials began to be used.

CHAPTER 7
APRÉS RACING: THE COWES WEEK EXPERIENCE ONSHORE

For visitors and spectators, Cowes Week is more than watching the sailing and catching some sun. Although a lot of the racing can be followed from the beach with the help of some good binoculars and an ear to the PA system, there's plenty of diversion elsewhere. Throughout the week, Cowes hosts a wide variety of street entertainment, harbour and marina events, live music and more. The historic and quaint old town of Cowes has plenty of "retail therapy" on offer and sailing fans have any number of opportunities to part with money in the numerous chandlery shops dotted up and down the cobbled high street. The main attraction is Cowes Yacht Haven where most of the black group racing yachts and many white group fleets are moored up on the floating pontoons.

After racing ends, late afternoon, the fleet heads in to the Yacht Haven – rush hour at the harbour. Crews hustle and scurry about their business, repairing, checking, rigging, discussing their day amid shouts of laughter, light-hearted abuse and team talks. Beers are cracked open on deck, food is grabbed – no time for lunch whilst racing. Food vendors and bars trade briskly amid a holiday atmosphere filled with a mixture of competitive camaraderie from the crews and bustle of onlookers. It's a pleasant surprise to find that there is very little of the "us" and "them" undercurrent that many competitive events seem to have – the sailing crews and the spectators mingle and mix, gossip, eat and drink, cram into the sailing shops, the inns and bars, the supermarket, the photo-galleries and the sailing clubs – everyone is welcome and of course anyone who enjoys sailing, has a boat and fancies a go, can compete. Cowes Week is a great spectator event because everyone's welcome to participate, get involved and feel a part of what's going on.

Visitors enjoy the hospitality of the iShares open-air bar during the Extreme 40 iShares Cup races.

Regatta House is the centre of operations during Cowes Week and where the daily results sheets are posted each afternoon. Crews soon gather to see how they're doing.

Crews chat outside Jolliffe's café, at the top of Cheapside. Joliffe's chandlery shop has moved across the street and the old place with its distinctively decorated shop-front now houses a coffee shop, which is said to be haunted by a mischievous little girl!

Cowes is an old and historic seaport town and as you might expect, preserves its history well. Dozens of historic houses, warehouses, sail lofts and customs buildings cluster around the old wharf. Narrow cobbled streets rise steeply from the mouth of the Medina, where a floating chain bridge links Cowes with East Cowes – where the Southampton ferry docks.

This page and opposite: *Local shops will do a brisk trade in Cowes Week souvenirs throughout the week whilst sponsors, tour operators, churches, pubs and eating houses will all do their best to enter into the spirit – and make some money too!*

Maritime art is plentiful in Cowes with artists setting up along the promenade on most days to try and capture something of the atmosphere.

Alum Bay and the Needles are the classic tourist destination for visitors to the Isle of Wight and with good reason during Cowes Week. Many of the black group races sail around the Needles and the viewpoint from the cliffs above Alum Bay makes a perfect spot to watch from – complete with picnic and powerful binoculars. After which, you can visit the famous Alum Bay chair lift down to the beach and buy a glass souvenir filled with the multi-coloured sands that form the crumbling cliffs here.

Opposite: Boatbuilding has been a mainstay of Cowes and the other Isle of Wight harbour towns for centuries and continues to thrive. Both new and historic boats are built, refurbished or restored, sometimes from the ground up, as with this hundred-year-old sloop undergoing a complete restoration by a single, skilled craftsman.

Egypt Point becomes a haven of peace and quiet from which to witness the often dramatic sunsets over the Solent, just as the nightlife gets underway in the packed town centre.

CHAPTER 8
HARBOUR LIFE: COWES WEEK
AWAY FROM THE RACING

The racing is competitive, hard fought, close run. Serious stuff for many of the owners and crews. Some of them are professional ocean racers with reputations to uphold, points to earn, money to make, sponsors to satisfy. But many are not. They came here for a good time, to sail, meet up with old friends, enjoy some competition, have a beer or two. For all of them, once the racing stops, the party can begin. There's time to relax, catch up with your mates, see how they got on out on the water. The Yacht Haven is the centre of things when the day's racing is over and there's plenty of activity, colour and spectacle to see as the big boats moor up and the crews get busy sorting out the tangle of sheets, lines and blocks ready for another day.

Opposite: *At the end of a hard day's racing you need to let your hair down.*

The crew of Charles Dunstone's class 1 winning TP2 off shore racer, Rio were joined by Simon LeBon for a day before heading back in for a well-earned rest.

The BT888 Open 60s crew relax on board and watch the final stages of the IRC class racing as they prepare the boat for the Fastnet race, which starts from Cowes immediately after the regatta finishes on the Sunday.

One of several international tall ships that make the journey over to support Cowes Week is JRR Tolkien. Built in 1964 the Tolkien is a luxurious gaff-topsail charter schooner.

Local boat, Helmi motors back into the Yacht Haven after a day's racing as the crew tidy up.

Opposite: Spectators who can get afloat will want to watch events from the water. Few will travel in quite as much style as in the steam yacht Kariat which makes a lovely sight pottering around the harbour.

Another great tradition of Cowes Week is the photography of Beken of Cowes. Several generations of the Beken family have been involved in photographing the event from 1888 onwards – about as long as the event's history itself. The Beken shop and gallery in Cowes is always busy with sailing fans looking for classic portraits of the great sailing boats of the past.

Rather less traditional sailing craft also appear, as sponsors try to attract attention.

Tuesday is Ladies Day and everyone gets into the spirit as Cowes Week celebrates the contribution that female sailors have made and continue to make to the sport.

Left: *Local fishing boats are pressed into service to offer rides out to the racing line.*

Pages 118–130: Cowes Yacht Haven comes alive as the fleet returns at the end of the day's racing. Now there's a chance for crews to catch up with each other, compare racing notes and discuss the wind and water conditions out there. There's plenty of activity throughout the Yacht Haven as gear is sorted and stowed, sails checked and repaired and friends and family come on board to see how the day has gone. Spectators have plenty of opportunity to get up close to the boats and crew and get a good view of what's going on.

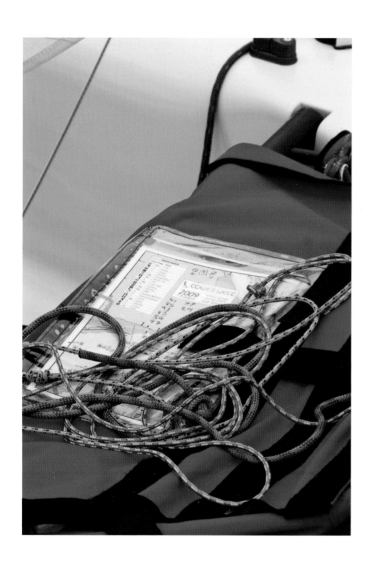

Pages 131–133: *One thing that doesn't change as Cowes Week gets underway, is the ferries: they come and go no matter what's going on or who's in the way, so skippers need to keep a wide berth and be aware – you don't want to hit one of these!*

CHAPTER 9
FIREWORKS NIGHT

Cowes Week is an event steeped in tradition and history and one of its defining highlights is fireworks night. This is a celebration that extends back to the very beginnings of Cowes Week. Fireworks night is not to be missed. Islanders and visitors alike begin to gather on the sea walls at East Cowes from late afternoon onwards even though the opening rocket won't go up until after dark. Street entertainers, bands, hot dog stands and ice cream vendors line the promenade road to service the gathering crowd.

At 7 o'clock the Red Arrows aerial display team scream overhead to the delight of the kids sitting on the harbour wall and the RNLI perform a simulated rescue out on the water. At 9.15pm the stewards, out on the floating pontoons determine that at last it's dark enough to light the fuses. The water is jammed with a flotilla of Ribs and powerboats vying for a grandstand view. When the fireworks go up it's worth the wait. The PA belts out Wagner and Beethoven and the sky and the water light up. It's great way to end the week.

Opposite: *The roads are closed by 6pm as everyone heads for East Cowes waterfront. This is a night even the local islanders have been waiting for.*

The Red Arrows perform a spectacular, ear-splitting display over Cowes Harbour as the crowds wait for darkness.

The RNLI put on a simulated air sea rescue display.

As the sun begins to set and evening shadows grow longer there is a growing sense of expectation for a great show on a perfect summer's evening.

A calm scene from the Royal Yacht Squadron as the moon rises over Cowes.

Finally, the first rocket is fired and everyone settles back to watch 30 minutes of spectacularly good fireworks light up the harbour-front in a tradition as old as Cowes Week itself, a fitting climax to a great British sporting event.

As daylight fades over the Isle of Wight's most famous landmark – the Needles – the lighthouse beams out its warning to shipping. The Solent is one of the busiest shipping channels in the world and a fitting home to the world's greatest sailing regatta – Cowes Week.

144